Dedication

To all those who ever struggled with learning a
foreign language and to Wolfgang Karfunkel

Also by Yatir Nitzany

Conversational Spanish Quick and Easy

Conversational Italian Quick and Easy

Conversational French Quick and Easy

Conversational Portuguese Quick and Easy

Conversational German Quick and Easy

Conversational Polish Quick and Easy

Conversational Russian Quick and Easy

Conversational Hebrew Quick and Easy

Conversational Yiddish Quick and Easy

Conversational Dutch Quick and Easy

Conversational Armenian Quick and Easy

Conversational Arabic Quick and Easy
Lebanese Dialect

Conversational Arabic Quick and Easy
Palestinian Dialect

Conversational Arabic Quick and Easy
Egyptian Dialect

Conversational Arabic Quick and Easy
Jordanian Dialect

Conversational Arabic Quick and Easy
Emirati Dialect

Conversational
Bulgarian
Quick and Easy

**THE MOST INNOVATIVE AND REVOLUTIONARY
TECHNIQUE TO MASTER CONVERSATIONAL BULGARIAN**

YATIR NITZANY

Foreword

About Myself

For many years I struggled to learn Spanish, and I still knew no more than about twenty words. Consequently, I was extremely frustrated. One day I stumbled upon this method as I was playing around with word combinations. Suddenly, I came to the realization that every language has a certain core group of words that are most commonly used and, simply by learning them, one could gain the ability to engage in quick and easy conversational Spanish.

I discovered which words those were, and I narrowed them down to three hundred and fifty that, once memorized, one could connect and create one's own sentences. The variations were and are *infinite*! By using this incredibly simple technique, I could converse at a proficient level and speak Spanish. Within a week, I astonished my Spanish-speaking friends with my newfound ability. The next semester I registered at my university for a Spanish language course, and I applied the same principles I had learned in that class (grammar, additional vocabulary, future and past tense, etc.) to those three hundred and fifty words I already had memorized, and immediately I felt as if I had grown wings and learned how to fly.

At the end of the semester, we took a class trip to San José, Costa Rica. I was like a fish in water, while the rest of my classmates were floundering and still struggling to converse. Throughout the following months, I again applied the same principle to other languages—French, Portuguese, Italian, and Arabic, all of which I now speak proficiently, thanks to this very simple technique.

This method is by far the fastest way to master quick and easy conversational language skills. There is no other technique that compares to my concept. It is effective, it worked for me, and it will work for you. Be consistent with my program, and you too will succeed the way I and many, many others have.

Contents

INTRODUCTION TO
THE PROGRAM

People often dream about learning a foreign language, but usually they never do it. Some feel that they just won't be able to do it while others believe that they don't have the time. Whatever your reason is, it's time to set that aside. With my new method, you will have enough time, and you will not fail. You will actually learn how to speak the fundamentals of the language—fluently in as little as a few days. Of course, you won't speak perfect Bulgarian at first, but you will certainly gain significant proficiency. For example, if you travel to Bulgaria, you will almost effortlessly be able engage in basic conversational communication with the locals in the present tense and you will no longer be intimidated by culture shock. It's time to relax. Learning a language is a valuable skill that connects people of multiple cultures around the world —and you now have the tools to join them.

How does my method work? I have taken twenty-seven of the most commonly used languages in the world and distilled from them the three hundred and fifty most frequently used words in any language. This process took three years of observation and research, and during that time, I determined which words I felt were most important for this method of basic conversational communication. In that time, I chose these words in such a way that they were structurally interrelated and that, when combined, form sentences. Thus, once you succeed in memorizing these words, you will be able to combine these words and form your own sentences. The words are spread over twenty pages. In fact, there are just nine basic words that will effectively build bridges, enabling you to speak in an understandable manner (please see Building Bridges). The words will also combine easily in sentences, for example, enabling you to ask simple questions, make basic statements, and obtain a rudimentary understanding of others' communications. I have also created Memorization-Made-Easy Techniques for this program in order to help with the memorization of the vocabulary.

My book is mainly intended for basic present tense vocal communication, meaning anyone can easily use it to "get by" linguistically while visiting a foreign country without learning the entire language. With practice, you will be 100 percent understandable to native speakers, which is your aim. One disclaimer: this is not a grammar book, though it does address minute and essential grammar rules (please keep your eyes peeled for grammar footnotes at the bottom of each and every page of the program). Therefore, understanding complex sentences with obscure words in Bulgarian is beyond the scope of this book.

People who have tried this method have been successful, and by the time you finish this book, you will understand and be understood in basic conversational Bulgarian. This is the best basis to learn not only the Bulgarian language but any language. This is an entirely revolutionary, no-fail concept, and your ability to combine the pieces of the "language puzzle" together will come with great ease, especially if you use this program prior to beginning a Bulgarian class.

This is the best program that was ever designed to teach the reader how to become conversational. Other conversational programs will only teach you phrases. But this is the only program that will teach you how to create your own sentences for the purpose of becoming conversational.

THE BULGARIAN LANGUAGE

Bulgarian is an Indo-European language and a member of the southern branch of the Slavic language family. It uses a Cyrillic alphabet and is spoken by over 8 million people mainly in Bulgaria, but also in Ukraine, Macedonia, Serbia, Turkey, Greece, Romania, Canada, USA, Australia, Germany, and Spain. Bulgarian is mutually intelligible with Macedonian, and fairly closely related to Serbian, Croatian, Bosnian, and Slovenian.

With the accession of Bulgaria to the European Union on 1 January 2007, Bulgarian is now also one of the official languages of the European Union.

Modern Bulgarian dates from the 16th century onwards and it underwent general grammar and syntax changes in the 18th and 19th centuries. Present-day written Bulgarian language was standardized after Bulgaria became independent in 1878 on the basis of the 19th-century Bulgarian vernacular. Many Turkish words were adopted into Bulgarian during the long period of Ottoman rule. Words have also been borrowed from Latin, Greek, Russian, French, Italian, German, and increasingly from English.

Spoken in: Bulgaria

MEMORIZATION MADE EASY

There is no doubt the three hundred and fifty words in my program are the required essentials in order to engage in quick and easy basic conversation in any foreign language. However, some people may experience difficulty in the memorization. For this reason, I created Memorization Made Easy. This memorization technique will make this program so simple and fun that it's unbelievable! I have spread the words over the following twenty pages. Each page contains a vocabulary table of ten to fifteen words. Below every vocabulary box, sentences are composed from the words on the page that you have just studied. This aids greatly in memorization. Once you succeed in memorizing the first page, then proceed to the second page. Upon completion of the second page, go back to the first and review. Then proceed to the third page. After memorizing the third, go back to the first and second and repeat. And so on. As you continue, begin to combine words and create your own sentences in your head. Every time you proceed to the following page, you will notice words from the previous pages will be present in those simple sentences as well, because repetition is one of the most crucial aspects in learning any foreign language. Upon completion of your twenty pages, congratulations, you have absorbed the required words and gained a basic, quick-and-easy proficiency and you should now be able to create your own sentences and say anything you wish in Bulgarian. This is a crash course in conversational Bulgarian, and it works!

NOTE TO THE READER

The purpose of this book is merely to enable you to communicate in Bulgarian. In the program itself (pages 16-40) you may notice that the composition of some of those sentences might sound rather clumsy. This is intentional. These sentences were formulated in a specific way to serve two purposes: to facilitate the easy memorization of the vocabulary and to teach you how to combine the words in order to form your own sentences for quick and easy communication, rather than making complete literal sense in the English language. So keep in mind that this is not a phrase book!

As the title suggests, the sole purpose of this program is for conversational use only. It is based on the mirror translation technique. These sentences, as well as the translations are not incorrect, just a little clumsy. Latin languages, Semitic languages, and Anglo-Germanic languages, as well as a few others, are compatible with the mirror translation technique.

Many users say that this method surpasses any other known language learning technique that is currently out there on the market. Just stick with the program and you will achieve wonders!

Again, I wish to stress this program is by no means, shape, or form a phrase book! The sole purpose of this book is to give you a fundamental platform to enable you to connect certain words to become conversational. Please also read the "Introduction" and the "About Me" section prior to commencing the program.

In order to succeed with my method, please start on the very first page of the program and fully master one page at a time prior to proceeding to the next. Otherwise, you will overwhelm yourself and fail. Please do not skip pages, nor start from the middle of the book.

It is a myth that certain people are born with the talent to learn a language, and this book disproves that myth. With this method, anyone can learn a foreign language as long as he or she follows these explicit directions:

* Memorize the vocabulary on each page

* Follow that memorization by using a notecard to cover the words you have just memorized and test yourself.

* Then read the sentences following that are created from the vocabulary bank that you just mastered.

* Once fully memorized, give yourself the green light to proceed to the next page.

Again, if you proceed to the following page without mastering the previous, you are guaranteed to gain nothing from this book. If you follow the prescribed steps, you will realize just how effective and simplistic this method is.

THE PROGRAM

Let's Begin! "Vocabulary"
(memorize the vocabulary)

I | I am	Az/ Az sum
With you	S teb
With him / with her	S nego / S neya
With us	S nas
For you	Za teb / (Plural) Za vas
Without him	Bez nego
Without them	Bez tyah
Always	Vinagi
Was	Beshe
This,	(Masc)Tozi, (fem) tazi, (neuter) tova, (Pl) tezi
You	(informal)Ti/ (formal) Vie/ (plural) Vie
Sometimes	Ponyakoga
Today	Dnes
Are you / you are	(informal)Si li/ti si (formal and plural)vie/vie ste
Better	Po-dobre
These	Tezi
He / She	Toi / Tya
From	*(from a place)* Ot, *(from person)* Ot
This is	(M) Tozi e/ (F) tazi e/ (N) tova e/ (Pl) tezi sa

Sentences from the vocabulary (now you can speak the sentences and connect the words)

I am always with her
Az sum vinagi s neya
This is for you
Tova e za teb
I am from Bulgaria
Az sum ot Balgaria
Are you from Sofia?
Ti ot Sofia li si?/
Vie ot Sofia li ste? (plural)

Sometimes you are with us at the mall
Ponyakoga ti si s nas v mola
I am with you
Az sum s teb /
Az sum s vas (plural)
Are you without them today?
Ti bez tyah li si dnes?
Sometimes I am with him
Ponyakoga az sum s nego

*Az sum is pronounced [az sə m]

*Bulgarian nouns have the categories grammatical gender, number, case (only vocative), and definiteness. A noun has one of three specific grammatical genders (masculine, feminine, neuter) and two numbers (singular and plural).

*In Bulgarian if the question doesn't have the question word: where, who, what, how, etc., you have to put the question particle *li* after the preposition, or the verb. It always goes together with the relevant auxiliary verb, for example **ti vie**. In the question, "**Are you** without them today?" you have to insert the particle *li* between "them" and "today" and to add a **si**, which is the auxiliary verb for "you" - *ti* - *Ti bez tyah **li si** dnes?* The word *li* does not mean anything by itself. It is only used to form questions.

16

I was	Az byah
To be	Da bada
Here	Tuk
Same	Sashto
Good/ Okay	Dobar (see footnote)
Day	Den
It's	To e
And	i
Between	Mezhdu
Now	Sega
Later / After	Po-kasno/ sled tova
If	Ako
Yes	Da
Then	Togava
Tomorrow	Utre
Very	Mnogo
Also/ too/ as well	Sashto

Between now and later
Mezhdu sega i po-kasno
If it's later, better tomorrow!
Ako e po-kasno, po-dobre utre!
This is also good
Tova sashto e dobre
It is the same
To e sashtoto
Yes, you are very good
Da, ti si mnogo dobar (M)/ dobra(F)
I was here with them
Az byah tuk s tyah
The same day
Sashtiyat den

*In Bulgarian, the definite article "the" doesn't exist as a separate word but as a suffix to the words. You should add the suffix -at, when the noun is a subject in the sentence, and as –a, when the word is not. In the case of our sentence, we translate "the mall" as mol-a.
*In Bulgarian you don't always use the full form "it's" / to e, but just "is" / e.
*There are three grammatical genders in Bulgarian: masculine (M), feminine (F) and neuter (N). The gender of the noun can largely be inferred from its ending: nouns ending in a consonant (zero ending) are generally masculine (for example, g rad – "city," sin – "son", mazh – "man". Those ending in –a/–ya, like zhena – "woman," dashterya –"daughter," are normally feminine. Nouns ending in –e, –o are almost always neuter dete – "child," ezero – "lake," as are those rare words (usually loanwords) that end in –i, –u, and –yu (tsunami – "tsunami," tabu – "taboo," menyu – "menu").
*In Bulgarian, to indicate "good" or "OK" we use dobar, however for (female) dobra, and (neuter) dobro.

Maybe	Mozhe bi
I go	Ti
Even if	Dazhe ako / dori ako
Afterwards	Posle / Sled tova
Worse	Po-losho
Where	Kade
Everything	(*person*)vseki,(*object*)vsichko
Somewhere	Nyakade
What	Kakvo?
Almost	Pochti
There	Tam

Afterwards is worse
Posle e po-losho
Even if I go now
Dori ako otida sega
Where is everything?
Kade e vsichko?
Maybe somewhere
Mozhe bi nyakade
Where are you?
Kade si ti?
You and I
Az i ti
What is this?
Kakvo e tova?
Where is the airport
Kade e letishteto?

*As mentioned earlier, in Bulgarian, the definite article "the" doesn't exist as a separate word but as a suffix. Because it's a word suffix, the definite article is also affected by the gender and ending of the word, and is different for different ones:

–*yat* and –*ya* for masculine gender (E.g. "the same day"/ *sashtiyat den*)
–*ta* for feminine gender (E.g. "the good book" / *dobrata kniga*)
–*to* for neuter gender (E.g. "the good child"/ *dobroto dete*)
–*te* for plural (E.g. "the good people"/ *dobrite hora*)

The definitive of "same" (*sashto*) is *sashtoto* (N), or *sashtiat* (M)/ *sushtata* (F). As you can see, it is affected by the gender and the ending of the word, and is different for the different ones.

House / home	Kashta / Dom
In / at	V / Na
Car	Kola/ Avtomobil
Already	Veche
Good morning	Dobro utro
How are you?	Kak si ti?
Where are you from?	Otkade si?
Me	Men
Hello / hi	Zdravei / Zdrasti
What is your name?	Kak se kazvash?/ kazvate? (formal)
How old are you?	Na kolko godini si?/godini ste?(Frml)
Son	Sin
Daughter	Dashterya
Your	Tvoy/vash (S,F);tvoite/ vashite (Pl)
But / however	No / Obache
Hard	Trudno (effort); Tvard (object)
Still	Vse oshte

She is without a car, maybe she is still at the house?
Tya e bez kola, mozhe bi tya e vse oshte v kashtata?
I am already in the car with your son and daughter
Az sum veche v kolata s tvoite sin i dashterya
Hello, what is your name?
Zdravei, kak se kazvash?
How old are you?
Na kolko si godini?
This is very hard
Tova e mnogo trudno
It's not impossible
To ne e nevazmozhno
Where are you from?
Otkade si?

*In Bulgarian there are three genders (as in Russian or German): masculine (*mazhki rod*), feminine (*zhenski rod*) and neuter (*sreden rod*). Every word has a gender and there are some rules for their determinations:
Masculine words end usually in a consonant, or in *iy*:
**mazh* /"a man," *valk* / "a wolf," *film*/ "a film," *geroiy*/ "a hero," *zhivot* / "a life"
But there are some words that end in –*A* or –*O*:
**bashta* / "a father," *chicho*/ "an uncle," *dyado* / "a grandfather," *sadia*/ "a judge," etc.
*Feminine words end usually in –*A*, –*Ya*, –*Ost*, –*Est*:
**zhena*/ "a woman," *masa*/ "a table," *kashta*/ "a house," *yabalka*/ "an apple," *staya*/ "a room," *radost*/ "joy," *bolest* / "an illness," etc.
There are a few exceptions that end in a consonant:
nosht / "a night," *krav* / "blood," *zahar* / "sugar," *sol* / "salt," *esen* / "autumn," etc.
The nouns that belong to the neuter gender have endings –*O*, –*E*, or end in E, I, U, Yu (the latter are usually loan words):
**momche* / "a boy," *momiche* / "a girl," *ezero* / "a lake," *litse* /"a face," *ime* / "a name"
**taksi* / "a taxi," *bizhu* / "a jewel," *menyu* / "a menu"
*Used definitive form. The word "house" – *kashta* is a feminine one, and gets its definite. form by adding -*ta*, *kashtata*.

Thank you	Blagodarya
For	Za
For (*a person*)	(a person) Za
That, that is	(M)Tozi e/(F)Tazi e/(N)Tova e/(P)Tezi sa
Time	Vreme
Our	Nashe
No	Ne
I am not	Az ne sum
Away	Navan/ Daleche
Late	Kasno
Similar	(M) Podoben (F) Podobna (N) Podobno
Other / Another	(M)Drug/(F)druga/(N)drugo/(P)drugi
Side	Strana
Until	Do
Yesterday	Vchera
Without us	Bez nas
Since	Ot
Not	Ne e
Before	Predi

Thanks for anything

Blagodarya za vsichko

I am not here, I am away

Az ne sum tuk, Az sum navan

That is a similar house

Tova e podobna kashta

I am from the other side

Az sum ot drugata strana

I was here last night

Az byah tuk predishnata nosht

*In Bulgarian the article "a" doesn't exist.

*Predishna means both "previous" and "former".

*This isn't a phrase book! The purpose of this book is *solely* to provide you with the tools to create *your own* sentences!

I say / I am saying	Kazvam/ Az kazvam
What time is it?	Kolko e chasat?
I want	Az iskam
Without you	Bez teb
Everywhere	Navsyakade
I go / I am going	Az otivam
With	S
My	Moi (male), moya (fem), moe (n), moite (pl)
Cousin	(M)Bratovched/(F)Bratovchedka
I need	Imam nuzhda ot
Right now	Tochno sega/ Vednaga
Night / evening	Nosht/ Vecher
To see	Da vidya
Light	Svetlina
Outside	Navan
I must	Az tryabva
During	Po vreme
I see / I am seeing	Az vizhdam
Happy	Shtastliv (M), shtastliva (F)
There	Tam

I am saying no / I say no
Az kazvam ne/ Kazvam ne
I want to see this in the day
Az iskam da vidya tova prez denya
I see this everywhere
Az vizhdam tova navsyakade
I am happy without my cousins here
Az sum shtastliv bez moite bratovchedi tuk
I need to be there at night
Az tryabva da bada tam prez noshta
I see light outside house
Az vizhdam svetlina izvan kashtata
What time is it right now?
Kolko chasa e tochno sega?

Tryabva means both "need" and "must;" both will be used interchangeably in this program.
*In Bulgarian, if it is about the time before 10 p.m. you should say *vecher* / "evening;" if it is after 10 p.m. - *nosht* / "night."
* *Prez* is an oft-used preposition in Bulgarian. It literally means "during."
*In Bulgarian, pronouns have different conjugations when relating to gender:
- "her"/ *neyno*, his/ *negovo*, its/ *negovo*, he/ *toi*, she/ *tya*, it/ *to*, they/ *te*
- "my"/ *moi* (male), *moya* (female), *moe* (neutral), *moite* (plural)
- "their"/ *tehen* (male), *tyahna* (female), *tyahno* (neutral), *tehnite* (plural)
- "your"/ *tvoy* (male), *tvoya* (female), *tvoe* (neutral), *tvoite* (plural)
- "your" (singular formal or plural)/ *vash* (male), *vasha* (fem), *vashe* (neuter), *vashi* (pl)
- "our"/ *nash* (male), *nasha* (female), *nashe* (neutral), *nashi* (plural)

Place	Myasto
Easy	Lesno
To find	Da namerya
To look for /to search	Da tarsya za
Near / Close	Nablizo/ Blizo
To wait	Da chakam
To sell	Da prodam
To use	Da izpolzvam
To know	Da znam
To decide	Da resha
Between	Mezhdu
Two	Dva (M)/Dve (F)
To	Da
That (*conjunction*)	Che

This place is easy to find
Tova myasto e lesno za namirane
I want to wait until tomorrow
Az iskam da chakam do utre
It's easy to sell this table
Lesno e da prodam tazi masa
I want to use this
Az iskam da izpolzvam tova
I want know where this house
Az iskam znam kade e tazi kashta
I need to know that everything is ok
Az tryabva da znam, che vsichko e nared

*In Bulgarian, you cannot start a sentence with an auxiliary verb, in this case "It's" / *e*, so the sentence starts with the adjective "Easy" / *lesno*, and the auxiliary verb goes after it: *Lesno e.*
*In the last sentence, "that" is used as a conjunction, *che*.

Because	Zashtoto
To buy	Da kupya
Both	I dvete
Them / They / Their	Tyah / Te / Tehen
Each / Every	Vseki / Kajd
Book	Kniga
Mine	Moi(M)/Moya(F)/Moe(N)/Moi(P)
To understand	Da razbera
Problem / Problems	Problem (S)/ problemi (P)
I do / I am doing	Pravya go / Az go pravya
Of	Kam
To look	Da gledam
Myself	Sebe si
Like this	Taka
Food	Hrana
Water	Voda
Hotel	Hotel
I like	Az haresvam

I like this hotel
Az haresvam tozi hotel
I want to look at the beach
Az iskam da gledam kum plazha
I want to buy a bottle of water
Az iskam da kupya butilka s voda
I do it like this each day
Az go pravya taka vseki den
That is the book, and that book is mine
Tova e knigata, I tazi kniga e moya
I need to understand the problem
Az tryabva da razbera problema
From the hotel I have a view of the city
Ot hotela az imam gledka kam grada
I can work today
Az moga da rabotya dnes
I do my homework
Az pravya moeto domashno

*Used definitive form. The word "book" – *kniga* in Bulgarian is a feminine one, and gets its definite form by adding the suffix *-ta, knigata.*
*With the knowledge you've gained so far, now try to create *your own* sentences!

There is / There are	Ima
Family	Semeistvo
Parents	Roditeli
Why	Zashto
To say	Da kazha
Something	Neshto
To go	Tragvam
Ready	Gotov
Soon	Skoro
To work	Da rabotya
Who	Koi
Important	Vazhno

I like to be at home with my parents

Az obicham da bada u doma s moite roditeli

I want to know why I must say something important

Az iskam da znam zashto tryabva da kazha neshto vazhno

I am there with him

Az sum tam s nego

I am busy, but I need to be ready soon

Az sum zaet, no tryabva da sum gotov skoro

I like to work

Az obicham da rabotya

Who is there?

Koi e tam?

I want to know if they are here, because I want to go outside

Az iskam da znam dali te sa tuk, zashtoto iskam da otida navan

There are seven dolls

Ima sedem kukli

I want to go to sleep

Az iskam da otida da spya

Az haresvam is a lighter form to express your love for something. When you want to express your deep personal and intimate love for something very close to you, like your home and parents, it's more appropriate to use the word in Bulgarian for "Love" / *Obicham*.

I love	Obicham
How much	Kolko
To take	Da vzema
With me	S men
Instead	Vmesto
Only	Samo
When	Koga
I can / Can I?	Az moga/ Moga li?
Or	Ili
Were	Kade
Without me	Bez men
Fast	Barzo
Slow	Bavno
Cold	Studeno
Inside	Vatre
To eat	Da yam
Hot	Goresht(M)/-ta(F); *(see footnote)*
To Drive	Da karam / Da shofiram

How much money do I need to take?
Kolko pari az tryabva da vzema?
Only when you can
Samo kogato ti mozhesh
They were without me yesterday
Te byaha bez men vchera
I need to drive the car very fast or very slowly
Az tryabva da karam kolata mnogo barzo ili mnogo bavno
It is cold in the library
Studeno e v bibliotekata
Yes, I like to eat this hot
Da, az obicham da yam tolkova lyuto

*In Bulgarian to indicate "hot" we use *goresht* (M); *-ta* (F); *to* (N) (for subject)/ *lyut* (M); *-ta* (F); *to* (N)(for food)

World	Sveta
To answer	Da otgovorya
To fly	Da letya
Yours	Tvoite
To travel	Da patuvam
To learn	Da ucha
Children	Detsa
To swim	Da pluvam
To practice	Da praktikuvam
To play	Da igraya
To leave	Da ostavya
Many/much/a lot	Mnogo
I go to	Otivam do
First	Parvo
Time / Times	Pati

I need to answer many questions
Tryabva da otgovorya na mnogo vaprosi
I want to fly today
Az iskam da letya dnes
I need to learn to swim
Az tryabva da se naucha da pluvam
I want to leave this here for you, when I go to travel the world
Az iskam da ostavya tova tuk za teb, kogato otida da patuvam po sveta
Since the first time
Ot parvia pat
The children are yours
Detsata sa tvoi
I need the books
Na men mi tryabvat knigite

*In Bulgarian, whenever pluralizing nouns, the ending changes to an *i*. For example, "book" / *kniga*, when pluralized, becomes *knigi*.
*With the knowledge you've gained so far, now try to create your own sentences!

Nobody	Nikoi
Against	Sreshtu
Us / we	Nas / nie
To visit	Da posetya
Mom / Mother	Mama/ maika
To give	Da dam
Which	Koito
To meet	Da sreshtna
Someone	Nyakoi
Just	Prosto
To walk	Da hodya
Around	Okolo
Family	Semeistvo
Than	Otkolkoto
Nothing	Nishto
Week	Sedmitsa

Something is better than nothing
Neshto e po-dobre ot nishto
I am against him
Az sum sreshtu nego
We go each week to visit my family
Nie hodim vsyaka sedmitsa da posetim moeto semeistvo
I need to give you something
Az tryabva da ti dam neshto
Do you want to meet someone?
Ti iskash li da sreshtnesh nyakogo?
I am here also on Wednesdays
Az sum tuk sashto v sryadite
You do this every day?
Ti pravish tova vseki den?
You need to walk around the house
Ti imash nuzhda da se razhojdash v kashtata

*In Bulgarian, the plurals of the names of the days are formed with the suffix – ite: *Ponedelnik – Ponedelnicite; Vtornicite; Sryadite; Chetvartacite; Petacite; Sabotite; Nedelite.*

I have	Az imam
Don't	Nedei
Friend	Priyatel
To borrow	Vzimam na zaem
To look like	Da izglezhdam kato
Grandfather	Dyado
To want	Da iskam
To stay	Da ostana
To continue	Da prodalzha
Way	Pat(*road*)/ nachin(*method*)
That's why	Eto zashto
To show	Da pokazha
To prepare	Da prigotvya
I am not going	Az nyama da hodya
How	Kak

Do you want to look like Arnold
Ti iskash li da izglezhdash kato Arnold
I want to borrow this book for my grandfather
Az iskam da vzema na zaem tazi kniga za moya dyado
I want to drive and to continue on this way to my house
Az iskam da karam I da prodalzha po tozi pat kam moyata kashta
I have a friend, that's why I want to stay with him in Sofia
Az imam priatel, eto zashto az iskam da ostana s nego v Sofia
I don't want to see anyone here
Az ne iskam da vizhdam nikoi tuk
I need to show you how to prepare breakfast
Nujno e da ti pokazha kak da prigotvish zakuska
Why don't you have the book?
Zashto nyamash knigata?
I don't need the car today
Az nyamam nuzhda ot kolata dnes

To remember	Da zapomnya
Bulgarian	Balgarski
Number	Nomer
Hour	Chas
Dark / darkness	Tamno / tamnina
About	Za
Grandmother	Baba
Five	Pet
Minute / Minutes	Minuta / minuti
More	Poveche
To think	Da mislya
To do	Da pravya
To come	Da doyda
To hear	Da chuvam
English	Angleren
To speak	Da govorya

I need to remember this number

Az tryabva da zapomnya tozi nomer

This is the last hour

Tova e poslednia chas

I want to hear my grandmother speak English today

Az iskam da chuya moyata baba da govori na angliyski dnes

I need to think more about this, and what to do

Az tryabva da pomislya poveche za tova, i kakvo da pravya

From here to there it's five minutes

Ot tuk do tam sa pet minuti

To leave	Da tragna
Again	Otnovo
Bulgaria	Balgaria
To bring	Da donesa
To try	Da opitam
To rent	Da naema
Without her	Bez neya
We are	Nie sme
To turn off	Da izklucha
To ask	Da pomolya
To stop	Da spra
Permission	Razreshenie

He needs to rent a house at the beach
Toi traybva da naeme kashta na moreto
Tonight I need to turn off the lights early
Dovechera az traybva da izgasya svetlinite rano
We want to stop here
Nie iskame da sprem tuk
We are from Plovdiv
Nie sme ot Plovdiv
The same building
Sashtata sgrada
I want to ask for permission to leave
Az iskam da pomolya za razreshenie da tragna
Can I leave?
Mozhe li az da tragna?

To open	Da otvorya
To buy	Da kupya
To pay	Da platya
Last	Posleden
Without	Bez
Sister	Sestra
To hope	Da se nadyavam
To live	Da zhiveya
Nice to meet you	Priyatno mi e da se zapoznaem
Name	Ime
Last name	Familiya
To return	Da se varna
Future	Badeshte
Door	Vrata
Our	Nash / nashata
On	Na

I need to open the door for my sister
Az tryabva da otvorya vratata za moyata sestra
I need to buy something
Az tryabva da kupya neshto
I want to get to know your sisters
Az iskam da se zapoznaya s tvoite sestri
Nice to meet you, what is your name and your last name?
Priyatno mi e da se zapoznaem, kak e tvoeto ime i tvoyata familia?
To hope for the better in the future
Da se nadyavame za po-dobro v badeshteto
Why are you sad right now?
Zashto si ti tazhen sega?
Our house is on the hill
Nashata kashta e na halma

*Sad = *tazhen* (M), *tazhna* (F), *tazhno* (N), *tazhni* (Plural)
*This *isn't* a phrase book! The purpose of this book is *solely* to provide you with the tools to create *your own* sentences!

To happen	Da se sluchi
To order	Da poracham
To drink	Da piya
Excuse me	Izvinete
Child	Dete
Woman	Zhena
To begin / To start	Da zapochna
To finish	Da svarsha
To help	Da pomogna
To smoke	Da pusha
To love	Da obicham
To talk / To Speak	Da govorya

This must happen today
Tova tryabva da se sluchi dnes
Excuse me, my child is here as well
Izvinete me, moeto dete e tuk sashto
I love you
Az te obicham
I see you
Az te vizhdam
I need you
Az se nuzhdaya ot teb
I want to help
Az iskam da pomogna
I don't want to smoke again
Az ne iskam da pusha otnovo
I want to learn to speak Bulgarian
Az iskam da se naucha da govorya Balgarski

Ot teb is the direct object pronoun of the pronoun "you."

To read	Da cheta
To write	Da pisha
To teach	Da prepodavam/ da obuchavam
To close	Da zatvorya
To turn on	Da vklyucha
To prefer	Da predpocheta
To put	Da slozha
Less	Po-malko
Sun	Slantse
Month	Mesets
I Talk	Az govorya
Exact	Tochno
To choose	Da izbera
In order to	Za da

I need this book, in order to learn how to read and write in Bulgarian
Tryabva mi tazi kniga, za da naucha kak da se cheta i pisha na Balgarski
I want to teach in Bulgaria
Az iskam da prepodavam v Balgaria
I want to close the door of the house and not to turn on the light
Az iskam da zatvorya vratata na kashtata i da ne vklyuchvam osvetlenieto
I prefer to put the gift here
Az predpochitam da slozha podaraka tuk
I want to pay less than you for the dinner
Az iskam da platya po-malko ot teb za vecheryata
I speak with the boy and the girl in Bulgarian
Az govorya s momcheto i momicheto na Balgarski
I see the sun today
Az vizhdam slanceto dnes
Is it possible to know the exact day?
Vazmozhno li e da se znae tochnia den?

To exchange	Da obmenya
To call	Da se obadya
Brother	Brat
Dad	Tatko / Bashta
To sit	Da sedna
Together	Zaedno
To change	Da se promenya
Of course	Razbira se
Welcome	(*read footnote*)
During	Po vreme na
Years	Godini
Sky	Nebe
Up	Nagore
Down	Nadolu
Sorry	Sazhalyavam
To follow	Da sledvam
Her	Tya
Big	Golyam
New	Nov
Never	Nikoga

I don't want to exchange this money at the bank
Az ne iskam da obmenya tezi pari v bankata
Today I want to call my brother and my dad
Dnes az iskam da se obadya na moya brat i na moya tatko
Of course I can come to the theater, and I want to sit together with you and with your sister
Razbira se, az moga da doida v teatara i iskam da sedna zaedno s teb i s tvoayata sestra.
I need to see your new house
Az tryabva da vidya tvoyata nova kashta
I can see the sky from the window
Az moga da vidya nebeto ot prozoreca

*In Bulgarian to indicate "welcome" we use *dobre doshal* (M) / *dobre doshla* (F) / *dobre doshlo* (N) / *dobre doshli* (Plural).

34

To allow	Pozvolyavam
To believe	Vyarvam
Morning	Utro
Except	S izklyuchenie na
To promise	Da obeshtaya
Good night	Leka nosht
To recognize	Da razpoznaya
People	Hora
To move	Dvizha se
To move *(to a place)*	Premestvam
Far	Daleche
Different	*(read footnote)*
Man	Mazh
To enter	Vlizam
To receive	Poluchavam
Tonight	Dovechera
Through	Chrez
Him / his	Nego / negovo

I believe everything except for this
Az vyarvam vsichko s izklyuchenie na tova
They need to recognize the Bulgarian people quickly
Te tryabva da razpoznayat Balgarskite hora barzo
I need to move your cat to another chair
Az tryabva da premestya tvoyata kotka na drug stol
I see the sun in the morning from the kitchen
Az vizhdam slanceto na sutrinta ot kuhnyata
I want his car
Az iskam tazi kola

*In Bulgarian to indicate "different" we use *drug / razlichen* (M) /
druga/ razlichna (F); *drugo/ razlicnno* (N); *drugi/ razlichni* (Plural).
*With the knowledge you've gained so far, now try to create your own
sentences!

To wish	Da pozhelaya
Bad	Losh
To Get	Da polucha
To forget	Da zabravya
Everybody / Everyone	(read footnote)
Although	Makar che
To feel	Chuvstvam
Great	Strahoten / Golyam
Next	Sledvasht
To like	Haresvam
In front	Otpred
Person	Chovek
Behind	Otzad
Well	Dobre
Goodbye	Dovizhdane
Restaurant	Restorant
Bathroom	Banya / Toaletna

I don't want to wish anything bad
Az ne iskam da pozhelaya nishto losho
I must forget everybody from my past
Az tryabva da zabravya vsichki ot moeto minalo
I am close to the person behind you
Az sum blizo do choveka zad teb
I say goodbye to my friends
Az kazvam dovizhdane na moite priateli
In which part of the restaurant is the bathroom?
V koya chast na restoranta e toaletnata?
I want a car before the next year
Az iskam kola predi sledvashtata godina
I like the house, however it is very small
Az haresvam kashtata, vapreki che e mnogo malka

*In Bulgarian to indicate "everybody" we use *vseki* (M)/ *vsyaka* (F) / *vsyako* (N)/ *vsichki* (Plural)

To remove	Da premahna
Please	Molya
Beautiful	(read footnote)
To lift	Povdigam
Include / Including	Vklyuchvam/vklyuchitelno
Belong	Prinadlezha
To hold	Da darzha
To check	Da proverya
Small	(read footnote)
Real	Istinski
Week	Sedmitsa
Size	Razmer
Even though	Makar che
Doesn't	Ne
So	Taka
Price	Tsena

She wants to remove this door
Tya iska da premahne tazi vrata
This doesn't belong here
Tova ne prinadlezhi tuk
I need to check again
Az tryabva da proverya otnovo
This week the weather was very beautiful
Tazi sedmica vremeto beshe mnogo hubavo
I need to know which is the real diamond
Az tryabva da znam koi e istinskiat diamant
We need to check the size of the house
Nie tryabva da proverim razmera na kashtata
I can pay this although the price is expensive
Az moga da platya tova, vapreki che tsenata e skapa
Is everything included in this price?
E li vsichko vklyucheno v tazi tsena?

*In Bulgarian, the verb "need" has two definitions: *tryabva* and *nuzhno*. Both signify doing something out of necessity such as "need to," "have to," "should." Both could be used interchangeably, however, *tryabva* has more of a colloquial use. On the other hand, *nuzhno* means "must;" something you are forced to do. You will notice in some instances, throughout the program, these two Bulgarian verbs being used interchangeably.
*In Bulgarian to indicate "small" we use *malak*(M)/*malka*(F)/*malko* (N)/*malki*(Pl).
*In Bulgarian to indicate "beautiful" we use *krasiv*(M)/*krasiva*(F)/*krasivo* (F)/ *krasivi*(Pl).

BUILDING BRIDGES

In Building Bridges, we take six conjugated verbs that have been selected after studies I have conducted for several months in order to determine which verbs are most commonly conjugated, and which are then automatically followed by an infinitive verb. For example, once you know how to say, "I need," "I want," "I can," and "I like," you will be able to connect words and say almost anything you want more correctly and understandably. The following three pages contain these six conjugated verbs in first, second, third, fourth, and fifth person, as well as some sample sentences. Please master the entire program up until *here* prior to venturing onto this section.

I want	Az iskam
I need	Az tryabva / Nuzhdaya se
I can	Az moga
I like	Az haresvam
I go	Az otivam
I have to/ I must	Az tryabva
To have	Imam

I want to go to my apartment
Az iskam da otida do moya apartament
I can go with you to the bus station
Az moga da otida s teb do avtobusnata spirka
I need to walk to the museum
Az tryabva da hodya do muzeya
I like the train
Az haresvam vlaka
I am want to teach a class
Az iskam da obuchavam klas
I have to speak to my teacher
Az tryabva da govorya s moya uchitel

Please master pages #16-#38, prior to attempting the following two pages!!

You want / do you want? – Ti iskash / Iskash li?
He wants / does he want? – Toi iska / Iska li toi?
She wants / does she want? – Tya iska / Iska li tya?
We want / do we want? – Nie iskame / Iskame li?
They want / do they want? – Te iskat / Iskat li?
You (plural/ formal sing) want – Vie iskate / Iskate li?

You need / do you need? – Ti imash nuzhda /Nuzhdaesh li se?
He needs / does he need? – Toi ima nuzhda/ Toi nuzhdae li se?
She needs / does she need? – Tya ima nuzhda/ Tya nuzhdae li se?
We Need / do we need? – Nie imame nuzhda / Nuzhdaem li se?
They need / do they need? – Te imat nuzhda / Nuzhdayat li se te?
You (plural/ formal sing) need – Vie imate nuzhda / Vie nuzhdaete li se?

You can / can you? - Ti mozhesh / Mozhesh li?
He can / can he? – Toi mozhe / Mozhe li?
She can / can she? – Tya mozhe / Mozhe li?
We can / can we? – Nie mozhem / Mozhem li?
They can / can they? – Te mogat / Mogat li?
You (plural/ formal sing) can – Vie mozhete / Mozhete li?

You like / do you like? – Ti haresvash / Haresvash li?
He likes / does he like? – Toi haresva / Haresva li toi?
She like / does she like? - Tya haresva / Haresva li tya?
We like / do we like? – Nie haresvame / Haresvame li?
They like / do they like? – Te haresvat / Haresvat li te?
You (plural/ formal sing) like – Vie haresvate / Haresvate li?

You go / do you go? – Ti otivash / Otivash li?
He goes / does he go? – Toi otiva / Toi otiva li?
She goes / does she go? – Tya otiva / Tya otiva li?
We go / do we go? – Nie otivame / Otivame li?
They go / do they go? – Te otivat / Otivat li?
You (plural/ formal sing) go – Vie otivate / Otivate li?

You must / do you have to - Ti tryabva / Tryabva li ti?
He must / does he have to – Toi tryabva / Toi tryabva li?
She must / does she have to - Tya tryabva / Tryabva li tya?
We have / do we have to - Nie tryabva / Tryabva li nie?
They must / do they have to - Te tryabva / Te tryabva li?
You (plural/ formal sing) must - Vie tryabva / Vie tryabva li?
You have - Ti tryabva / Tryabva li ti?

He has – Toi ima
She has – Tya ima
We have – Nie imame
They have – Te imat
You (plural) have – Vie imate

Please master pages #16-#39, prior to attempting the following page!!

Do you want to go?
Iskash li da otidesh?
Does he want to fly?
Toi iska li da leti?
We want to swim
Nie iskame da pluvame
Do they want to run?
Te iskat li da byagat?
Do you need to clean?
Ti tryabva li da chistish?
She needs to sing a song
Tya ima nuzhda da pee pesen
We need to travel
Nie tryabva da patuvame
They don't need to fight
Te ne sa dlazhni da se karat
You (plural) need to see the film
Vie tryabva da gledate filma
Can you hear me?
Mozhesh li da me chuesh?
He can dance very well
Toi mozhe da tantsuva mnogo dobre
We can go out tonight
Nie mozhem da izlezem dovechera
They can break the wood
Te mogat da schupyat darvoto
Do you like to eat here?
Haresva li ti da yadesh tuk?

He likes to spend time here
Toi obicha da prekarva vreme tuk
We like to fix the house
Nie haresvame da remontirame kashtata
They like to cook
Te obichat da gotvyat
You (plural) like my house
Vie haresvate moyata kashta
Do you go to school today?
Shte hodish li na uchilishte dnes?
He goes fishing
Toi hodi za riba
We are going to relax
Nie otivame da si pochinem
They go to watch a film
Te otivat da gledat film
Do you have money?
Imash li pari?
She must look outside
Tya tryabva da pogledne otvan
We have to sign here
Nie tryabva da podpishem tuk
They have to send the letter
Te tryabva da izpratyat pismoto
You (plural) have to order
Vie tryabva da porachate

Days of the Week

Sunday	Nedelya
Monday	Ponedelnik
Tuesday	Vtornik
Wednesday	Sryada
Thursday	Chetvartak
Friday	Petak
Saturday	Sabota

Seasons

Spring	Prolet
Summer	Lyato
Autumn	Esen
Winter	Zima

Cardinal Directions

North	Sever
South	Yug
East	Iztok
West	Zapad

Colors

Black	Cheren (M)/ Cherna (F)/ Cherno (N)/ Cherni(Pl)
White	Byal (M)/ Byala (F)/ Byalo (N)/ Beli (Pl)
Gray	Siv (M)/ Siva(F)/ Sivo(N)/ Sivi (Pl)
Red	Cherven (M)/ Chervena (F)/ Cherveno (N)/ Cherveni (Pl)
Blue	Sin (M)/ Sinya (F)/ Sinyo (N)/ Sini (Pl)
Yellow	Zhalt (M)/ Zhalta (F)/ Zhalto (N)/ Zhalti (Pl)
Green	Zelen (M)/ Zalena (F)/ Zeleno (N)/ Zeleni (Pl)
Orange	Oranzhev(M)/Oranzheva(F)/Oranzhevo (N)/Oranzhevi(Pl)
Purple	Lilav (M)/ Lilava (F)/ Lilavo(N)/ Lilavi (Pl)
Brown	Kafyav (M)/ Kafyava (F)/ Kafyavo (N)/ Kafyavi (Pl)

Numbers

One	Edno
Two	Dve
Three	Tri
Four	Chetiri
Five	Pet
Six	Shest
Seven	Sedem
Eight	Osem
Nine	Devet
Ten	Deset

CONGRATULATIONS, NOW YOU ARE ON YOUR OWN!

If you merely absorb the required three hundred and fifty words in this book, you will then have acquired the basis to become conversational in Bulgarian! After memorizing these three hundred and fifty words, this conversational foundational basis that you have just gained will trigger your ability to make improvements in conversational fluency at an amazing speed! However, in order to engage in quick and easy conversational communication, you need a special type of basics, and this book will provide you with just that.

Unlike the foreign language learning systems presently used in schools and universities, along with books and programs that are available on the market today, that focus on *everything* but being conversational, *this* method's sole focus is on becoming conversational in Bulgarian as well as any other language. Once you have successfully mastered the required words in this book, there are two techniques that if combined with these essential words, can further enhance your skills and will result in you improving your proficiency tenfold. *However* , these two techniques will only succeed *if* you have completely and successfully absorbed the three hundred and fifty words. *After* you establish the basis for fluent communications by memorizing these words, you can enhance your conversational abilities even more if you use the following two techniques.

The first step is to attend a Bulgarian language class that will enable you to sharpen your grammar. You will gain additional vocabulary and learn past and present tenses, and if you apply these skills that you learn in the class, together with the three hundred and fifty words that you have previously memorized, you will be improving your conversational skills tenfold. You will notice that, conversationally, you will succeed at a much higher rate than any of your classmates. A simple second technique is to choose Bulgarian subtitles while watching a movie. If you have successfully mastered and grasped these three hundred and fifty words, then the combination of the two—those words along with the subtitles—will aid you considerably in putting all the grammar into perspective, and again, conversationally, you will improve tenfold.

Once you have established a basis of quick and easy conversation in Bulgarian with those words that you just attained, every additional word or grammar rule you pick up from there on will be gravy. And these additional words or grammar rules can be combined with the three hundred and fifty words, enriching your conversational abilities even more. Basically, after the research and studies I've conducted with my method over the years, I came to the conclusion that in order to become conversational, you first must learn the words and then learn the grammar.

The Bulgarian language is compatible with the mirror translation technique. Likewise, with this language, you can use this mirror translation technique in order to become conversational, enabling you to communicate even more effortlessly. Mirror translation is the method of translating a phrase or sentence, word for word from English to Bulgarian, by using these imperative words that you have acquired through this program (such as the sentences I used in this book. Latin languages, Middle Eastern languages, and Slavic languages, along with a few others, are also compatible with the mirror translation technique. Though you won't be speaking perfectly proper and precise Bulgarian, you will still be fully understood and, conversation-wise, be able to get by just fine.

CONCLUSION

Congratulations! You have completed all the tools needed to master the Bulgarian language, and I hope that this has been a valuable learning experience. Now you have sufficient communication skills to be confident enough to embark on a visit to Bulgaria, impress your friends, and boost your resume so good luck.

This program is available in other languages as well, and it is my fervent hope that my language learning programs will be used for good, enabling people from all corners of the globe and from all cultures and religions to be able to communicate harmoniously. After memorizing the required three hundred and fifty words, please perform a daily five-minute exercise by creating sentences in your head using these words. This simple exercise will help you grasp conversational communications even more effectively. Also, once you memorize the vocabulary on each page, follow it by using a notecard to cover the words you have just memorized and test yourself and follow that by going back and using this same notecard technique on the pages you studied during the previous days. This repetition technique will assist you in mastering these words in order to provide you with the tools to create your own sentences.

Every day, use this notecard technique on the words that you have just studied.

Everything in life has a catch. The catch here is just consistency. If you just open the book, and after the first few pages of studying the program, you put it down, then you will not gain anything. However, if you consistently dedicate a half hour daily to studying, as well as reviewing what you have learned from previous days, then you will quickly realize why this method is the most effective technique ever created to become conversational in a foreign language. My technique works! For anyone who doubts this technique, all I can say is that it has worked for me and hundreds of others.

Note from the Author

Thank you for your interest in my work. I encourage you to share your overall experience of this book by posting a review. Your review can make a difference! Please feel free to describe how you benefited from my method or provide creative feedback on how I can improve this program. I am constantly seeking ways to enhance the quality of this product, based on personal testimonials and suggestions from individuals like you.

Thanks and best of luck,

Yatir Nitzany

Made in the USA
Middletown, DE
20 May 2021